GABI'S FABULOUS FUNCTIONS

written by Caroline Karanja

illustrated by Ben Whitehouse

Meet our coding creatives!

This is Adi. Adi likes arts and crafts. She spends most of her time coloring, playing music, and making things. Whenever she sees something new, she wonders how it came to be. She likes to say, "I wonder . . ."

This is Gabi. Gabi loves to read, play outside, and take care of her dog, Charlie. She is always curious about how things work. Whenever she sees something that needs fixing, she tries to find the best way to improve it. She often says, "What if . . .?"

Adi and Gabi make a great team!

Gabi and her mom are grocery shopping. They are buying ingredients that Gabi and Adi will need for some recipes. Recipes are instructions that lead to an end result: something delicious!

blueberries + strawberries + bananas = fruit salad
tomatoes + green peppers + lime juice + cilantro = salsa

Today is Gabi's father's birthday. Gabi wants to make him breakfast. Adi has come over to help.

Gabi's mom had to go to work. Before she left, she prepared the ingredients for fruit salad and breakfast tostadas.

"Let's start with the fruit salad," Adi says. "It's the easiest."

"Here's what we need," Gabi says, reading the recipe. "Blueberries, strawberries . . ."

"Mixing ingredients to make something new is like a function in computer programming," Adi says. "When you ask for a cookie, you don't say, 'Please pass the eggs and flour and sugar and butter and chocolate chips.' You just say, 'Pass the cookies, please!'"

"A function is like a recipe for a computer!" Gabi says. "It tells the computer that when you say 'cookie,' what you really mean is: eggs, flour, sugar, butter, and chocolate chips all mixed and baked into circle shapes."

Functions

A function is a block of code that performs a certain task. It tells a computer what you need it to do, without having to explain every step. Functions help programmers avoid having to repeat the same actions over and over. If you need to do a task again and again, you can create a function that works as a shortcut. Functions have an input (like the ingredients) and an output (like the cookie).

"Instead of fruit salad, how about if we make a parfait?" Adi suggests.

"What's a parfait?" Gabi asks.

"It's made with yogurt, berries, and granola. Since we already have berries, we just need some yogurt and granola," Adi says.

Gabi checks the refrigerator. "We have those."

"Great!" Adi says. She puts some yogurt in a bowl and adds some berries.

Then Gabi adds a sprinkle of granola. "All done!"

Gabi picks up the tostada recipe. "So if recipes are like functions, the input for this would be: refried beans, grated cheese, avocado, lettuce, salsa, and a corn tortilla," she says.

Adi and Gabi put together the tostada using the ingredients Gabi's mother prepared.

"And the output is the tostada!" Adi cheers. "Now we just need to warm it up."

"Let's make some more parfaits," Gabi says. "What if we make a function factory? A parfait function factory!"

The girls make a sign that says *input*. They put it next to the ingredients sitting on the counter: yogurt, berries, and granola. Then they make a sign that says *output* for the finished parfaits.

Between the two signs, they set up a box that says *function*.

"When we input the ingredients, our output will be a parfait!" Gabi says.

Functions in a Video Game

In a video game, you might want to make your character run, jump, or turn. Several code blocks would be needed to make each of those actions (or tasks) happen. The code blocks need to appear in a certain order to make the task(s) happen correctly. Instead of typing out all those code blocks every time, you could create a function for each task. A function combines many steps into one. The code blocks are the inputs for your function. The action is the output.

You could name your functions: RUN, JUMP, TURN LEFT, or TURN RIGHT. The functions might look like this:

$$\text{code a} + \text{code b} + \text{code a} = \text{RUN}$$
$$\text{code c} + \text{code d} = \text{JUMP}$$
$$\text{code e} + \text{code f} = \text{TURN LEFT}$$
$$\text{code e} + \text{code g} = \text{TURN RIGHT}$$

Each function would run the code blocks needed for that task. That way, with just one click, your character can run, jump, or turn quickly to win the game!

Gabi's dad comes into the kitchen.

"Happy birthday!" Gabi and Adi call out.

"We used functions to make your breakfast," Gabi explains.

"Let's show your dad our parfait function factory!" Adi says.

"OK, I'll be the computer," Gabi says. She stands behind the box so that her dad can't see what she's doing. "Input, please!" she says to Adi.

Adi hands her the yogurt, berries, and granola. Behind the box, Gabi quickly mixes the ingredients into a fancy glass to make a parfait. Then she sets the finished parfait next to the output sign.

OutPut

Ding! goes the toaster oven.

"Now your tostada is ready too!" Gabi says. She carefully puts it on a plate and gives it to her dad. Adi hands him his parfait.

Gabi's dad dips a spoon into the parfait and takes a bite.
"Well, this is the most delicious 'output' I've ever had!" he
says. "Good coding—and cooking—girls!"

Which function makes the perfect pizza?

Adi and Gabi decide to make a pizza for lunch. The ingredients—or input—for their pizza are cheese, sauce, dough, and pepperoni. Just like code blocks in a function, ingredients need to go in a certain order to get the right result. Which row shows the correct order to get the right results for a pizza?

 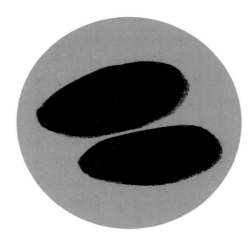 

  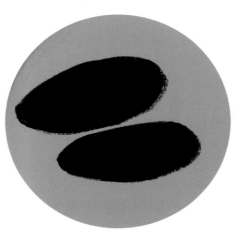

Glossary

code—one or more rules or commands to be carried out by a computer

code block—a set of code that is grouped together

computer—an electronic machine that can store and work with large amounts of information

function—a set of steps or instructions that together create a specific result

input—a command that is entered

output—the result of a specific set of commands and steps being entered

programmer—a person who writes code that can be run by a machine

task—a piece of work that needs to be done

Think in Code!

- Think of your favorite game. Can you write the function or set of instructions for playing the game?
- Come up with a function to make your favorite sandwich. Don't forget to include all the inputs—or your output won't come out right!
- See how many functions you can find in your day. Did you make a craft? Make a bowl of cereal? Those are functions! What other functions can you think of?

About the Author

Caroline Karanja is a developer and designer who is on a mission to increase accessibility and sustainability through technology. She enjoys figuring out how things work and sharing this knowledge with others. She lives in Minneapolis.

This book is dedicated to Anaïs
for your friendship and encouragement —C. K.

Picture Window Books are published by Capstone
1710 Roe Crest Drive, North Mankato, Minnesota 56003
www.mycapstone.com

Library of Congress Cataloging-in-Publication data is available on the Library of Congress website.

978-1-5158-3444-1 (paper over board)
978-1-5158-2743-6 (library hardcover)
978-1-5158-2747-4 (paperback)
978-1-5158-2751-1 (eBook PDF)

Summary: Two friends explore how functions used in computer programming can
also be used in their everyday lives—especially in the kitchen!

Editor: Kristen Mohn
Designer: Kay Fraser
Design Element: Shutterstock/Arcady

Printed and bound in the United States of America.
PA021

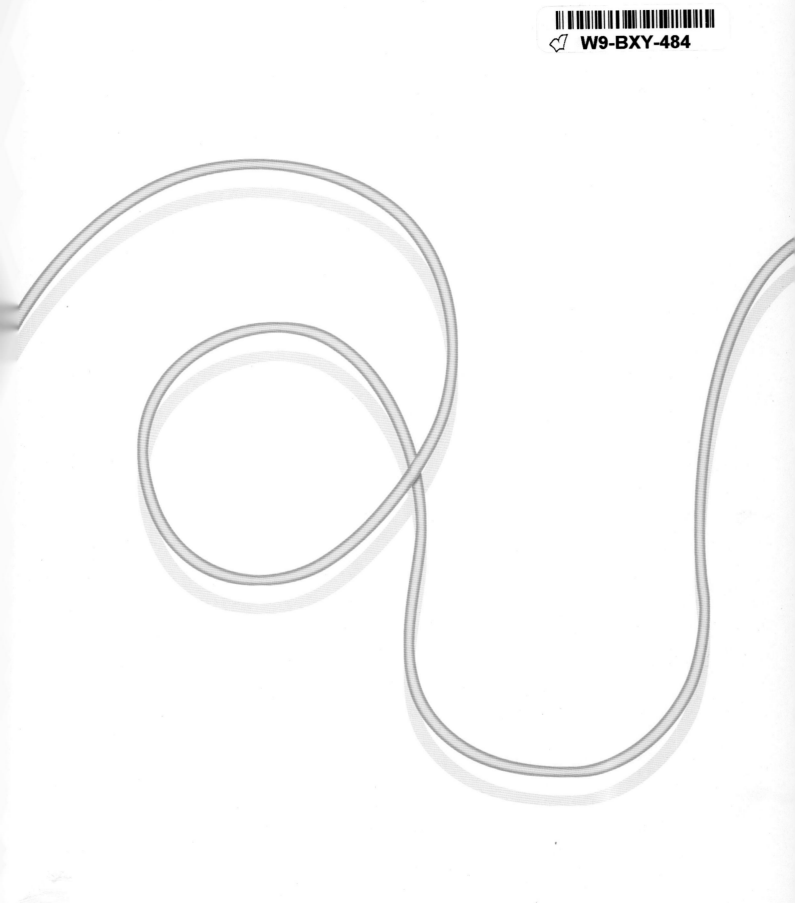

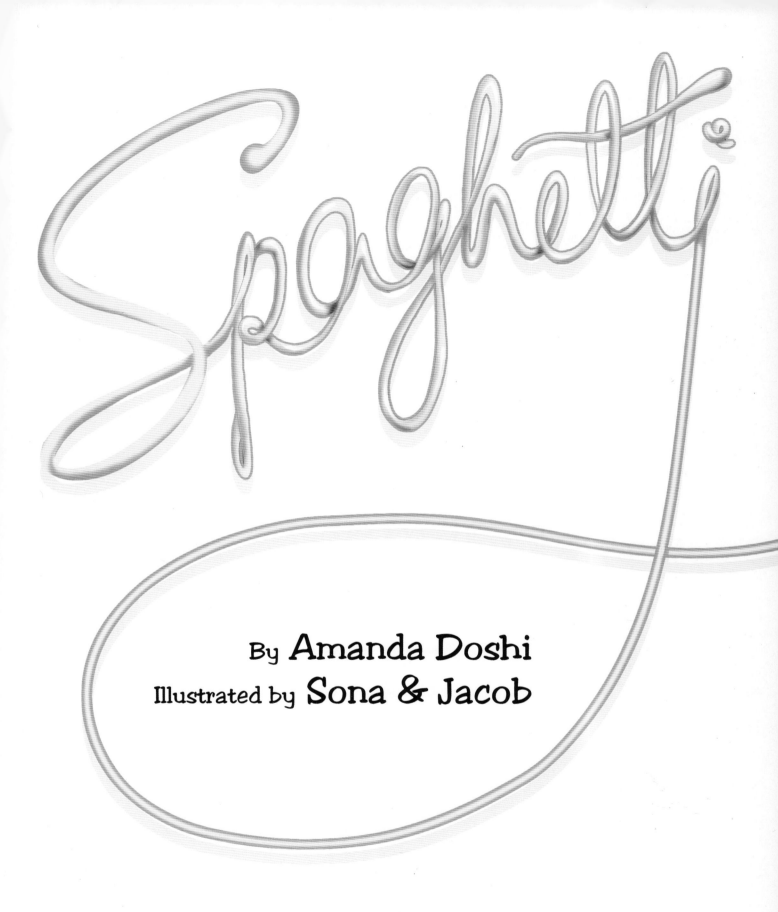

Spaghetti

By Amanda Doshi

Illustrated by Sona & Jacob

For Amara Eden, my Anam Cara

- A.D.

Whirling Dervish LLC
whirlingdervishpress.com

LCCN 2010921425 ~ ISBN 978-0-9844412-0-4

Printed in India

My name is Freddy. My favorite food is spaghetti. I like to eat my noodles by slurping them up one at a time. The really long noodles are the best. If I could make spaghetti, I would make a noodle SO long that it would stretch all the way around the world!

First, my spaghetti noodle would stretch down the street, across the San Francisco Bay and under the Golden Gate Bridge. The color of the bridge is "International Orange," and painters touch up the paint all year long. I saw them once when I was driving over the bridge with my family.

Then it would cross the Pacific Ocean down to the Sydney Opera House in Australia. The architect of the Opera House wanted the roof to look like ship sails blowing in the wind. I think he did a great job!

It would stretch along the Great Wall of China. People used to say that you could see the Great Wall from the moon. That's not true, but you can see it from the International Space Station.

My spaghetti would visit the Taj Mahal in India. Do you know it took 22,000 workers and 1,000 elephants 22 years to build the Taj Mahal? That makes homework sound easy!

My noodle would climb over the summit of Mt. Everest - the tallest mountain on earth! It is on the border of Nepal and Tibet. The Nepalese name for the mountain is Sagarmatha, and the Tibetan name is Chomolungma. Say that three times really fast!

Then it would twist around Saint Basil's Cathedral in Russia.
When the church was built, the domes were gold. Over time they
were painted in many bright colors. I think they look like candy!

My spaghetti would slide over the boulders of Stonehenge in England. Stonehenge is a big mystery - no one knows how it was built or why it is there. Some people even think aliens built it. How cool would that be?

It would climb to the top of the Eiffel Tower in France. There are two restaurants in the Eiffel Tower. People would have to be very careful not to drop any food!

It would weave through the pillars of the Parthenon in Greece.
The Parthenon was built for the goddess Athena. She was strong
and wise and protected the Greeks in all their battles.

My noodle would zoom past the Great Pyramids of Giza in Egypt. Khufu's pyramid was the tallest building on earth for almost five thousand years, until the Eiffel Tower was built.

It would fly through the mist of Victoria Falls. The falls are in both Zimbabwe and Zambia. They were named after Queen Victoria, but she never got to visit them.

Then it would cross the Atlantic Ocean to the Emperor Penguins of Antarctica. Emperors are the biggest penguins of all. They can weigh almost 90 pounds - that's bigger than me!

Next, my noodle would adventure through the jungles of the Amazon. About HALF of all the animals on earth live in rainforests. That's why we have to take good care of them.

Then it would wrap around the Statue of Liberty in New York. The seven rays of Lady Liberty's crown represent the seven continents of the world... every place my noodle visited!

Finally, my spaghetti noodle would land on my plate.
I would take one HUGE slurp,

and the end of the noodle would zip
all the way back...

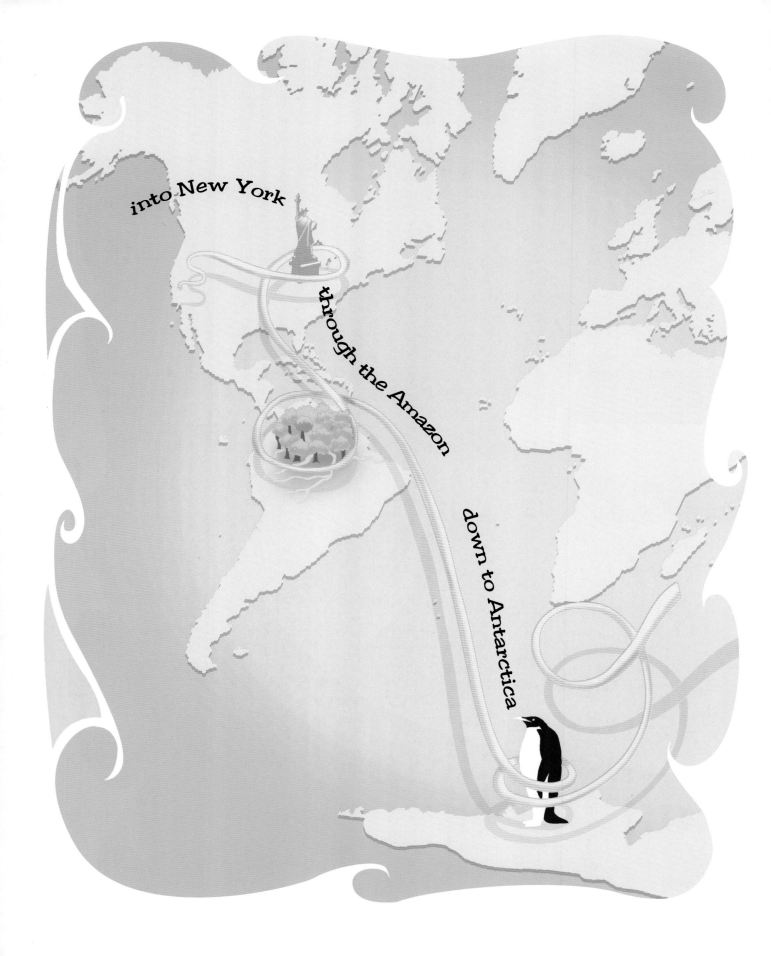

into New York

through the Amazon

down to Antarctica

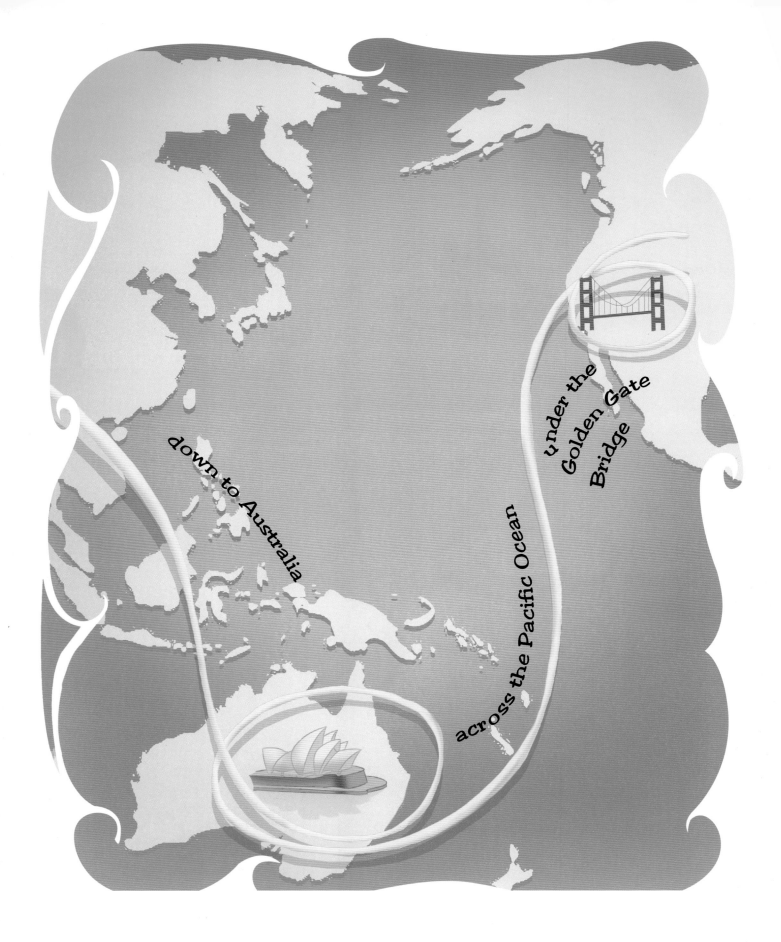

onto my plate and into my mouth!
YUM!